CANDLE CRAFTS

To Carla and Ezio

A warm thank you to:
Maurizio Minora, Lella Galli, Anna Giulietti, Nicoletta Romanelli, Chiara Gelmetti

Osvaldo D'Amore, for his beautiful candles, every evening in Brera
(L-c-d-O@hycosmail.com)

HABITAT, via Ripamonti 89, Milan
URUSHI, c.so Garibaldi 65, Milan
MOSAIQUE, via Castelfidardo 2, Milan
LES MAGIES, via Goito 5, Milan
TAD, via Croce Rossa 1, Milan
Author's e-mail address: paolarom@katamail.com

Editor-in-chief: *Cristina Sperandeo*
Photograhy: *Alberto Bertoldi*
Translation: *Chiara Tarsia*
Graphic layout: *Paola Masera and Amelia Verga with Beatrice Brancaccio*

Library of Congress Cataloging-in-Publication Data Available

10 9 8 7 6 5 4 3 2 1

Published by Sterling Publishing Company, Inc.
387 Park Avenue South, New York, NY 10016
First published in Italy by RCS Libri S.p.A.
under the title *Candele per ogni occasione*
© 1999 RCS Libri S.p.A., Milan 1st Edition Great Fabbri Manuals September 1999
© 2001 English translation by Sterling Publishing Co., Inc.
Distributed in Canada by Sterling Publishing Co., Inc.
C/o Canadian Manda Group, One Atlantic Avenue, Suite 105
Toronto, Onatario, Canada M6K 3E7
Distributed in Great Britain and Europe by Cassell PLC
Wellington House, 125 Strand, London WC2R 0BB, England
Distributed in Australia by Capricorn Link (Australia) Pty Ltd.
P.O. Box 704, Windsor, NSW 2756, Australia

Sterling ISBN 0-8069-7605-5

Paola Romanelli

CANDLE CRAFTS

Sterling Publishing Co., Inc.
New York

TABLE OF CONTENTS

INTRODUCTION. 6

BASIC TECHNIQUE 9

Materials. 10
Equipment 12
Preparing Wax 15
Useful Tips 16
The Wick 18
Scenting Wax 21

MAKING CANDLES 23

Dipped Candles 24
Twisted Candles 30
Beeswax 32
Rainbow Candles 36

CANDLES IN MOLDS 43

Molds. 44
Rubber Molds 46
Plastic Molds 50
Geometrical Shapes 54
Kitchen Molds 60
Floating Candles 62
Ice Cubes. 64
Making Molds 66

CANDLE-HOLDERS 71

Terracotta Vases 72
Using Sand 78
Shell Holders 82
Holders from Natural Products 84
A Silver Glow 88
Magic Lanterns 92
Candles Made with Unheated Wax 96

DECORATED CANDLES 101

Dried Flowers 102
Carved Candles 108
Tempera Decorations 110
Stamped Candles 112
Decorating with Sponges 116
Stencil Motifs 120
Silver and Gold Decorations 122
Delightful Transfers 124
Advent Candles 126
Wax Applications 128
Ribbons 132
Seed Coated Candles 136
Enfolded in Nature 140
Corrugated Cardboard 146
Engraved Candles 148
Paper Lanterns 150

CANDLES FOR EVERY OCCASION 153

Easter 154
Christmas 154
Saint Valentine's Day 156
Halloween 156
Birthdays 158
INDEX 160

INTRODUCTION

From the earliest times, man has been interested in lighting candles. The motives that have driven him to perform this simple action have always been manifold. Candles are lit to gain light, to create an ambience for meditation purposes, and as a part of many traditions of prayer.

In our culture, candles have gradually come to assume the value of a time clock; Think of the candles on a birthday cake, more and more numerous as the years go by; of the white candles mixed with the scent of incense which accompany Christening and Confirmation ceremonies, of the red and gold candles which bedeck the home at Christmas, of the elegant candles which embellish the table during important dinners and lastly, of the large candles burning during the wake at the moment of death.

During every one of these moments, the ritual of lighting a candle can capture a person's imagination completely, with even hypnotic effects on some.

When snuffing out a candle ask of the burning candle happiness, comfort, love and eternal peace for oneself and one's loved ones. Those who believe in magic practices maintain that it is fundamental to make the candles themselves for each ritual, because candles feel the influence of those manipulating them.

Making candles oneself is important because nothing can influence your candle but you. Nothing can come between you and the candle. The candle must be manipulated only by the person who will draw benefit from it, and must be made bearing in mind the use for which it is intended. And now, after all of this academic talk, let's get down to it!

BASIC TECHNIQUE

MATERIALS

The most important ingredient in candle making is wax, which is available on the market in different forms:

– *Beeswax:* a substance secreted by honeybees for constructing beehives. It is gathered from the honeycombs, which makes up the cells, and is then melted in water. It can be found in sheets, sticks, and small beads. Of all the waxes, beeswax is the most expensive and difficult to find.

– *Paraffin:* a mix of solid hydrocarbon available from natural deposits or derived from crude oil. It is of a white, translucent color. Its specific weight is less than that of water, with which it doesn't mix. The ideal temperature for melting paraffin varies between 120 and 175 °F. It is available on the market in flakes or slabs; it is cheap and easy to work. White or transparent candles can be made with paraffin wax.

– *Stearin:* a mix of acid fats, particularly suitable for making wax if added to paraffin. If you make a candle that is 20% stearin and 80% paraffin, it reduces candle dripping considerably, makes it easier to dye the candle and to extract it from the mold, renders its color opaque, and diminishes the smoke it creates. It is available in powder or in very small grains. In some places, a mix for candles, made up of the right proportions of paraffin and stearin is available commercially in packages of 2-10 pounds.

– *Wick:* a cord of twisted or woven fibers making up the core of the candle. The size of a wick is important: if it is too big compared to the candle, the flame will create a lot of smoke. On the other hand, if it is too small, the wick will probably drown in the wax.

EQUIPMENT

– To melt wax bains-marie style, use a kitchen pot, about 8" wide, that can hold several pots containing different colored waxes.

– Molten wax can be placed in a variety of containers: glass, such as jam jars or laboratory beakers, which have the advantage of a small neck for pouring, ordinary, everyday pots, or in heat-proof plastic bags.

– A funnel, of glass if possible, is indispensable for pouring wax into molds, especially because of its narrow-neck.

– The sealer is a paste which, when kneaded, becomes soft. It is used to seal the molds, and to secure the wick to the base of the molds to prevent it from moving.

– Use wooden skewers to secure the wick to the mold. Their length makes it possible to rest them on the edges of the mold.

– Glue for wax is available on the market. It must be heated before being applied to the candle.

– A cutter, necessary for trimming the candle.

– A pair of sharp scissors.

Beaker

Funnel

Scissors

Skewers

Sealer

Pot for heating wax
bains-marie style

Glue

Cutter

PREPARING WAX

Only a few simple operations are needed to make wax with powdered stearin and paraffin. Pour the paraffin into a heat-resistant glass container and then stearin to the equivalent of 10-20% of the total.

Heat the mixture bains-marie style and mix with a wooden spoon.

Every now and again measure the temperature, until the mixture reaches melting point (284°F – 347°F) and the wax becomes liquid and transparent. Take the container off your heat source.

USEFUL TIPS

To dye candles, add some powdered wax dye to the molten wax and mix it with a spoon. Then pour some colored wax on a white surface and wait until it cools down; at that point you can discern its true hue. When cooled, wax tends to slightly change color.

Wax is flammable, therefore be very careful when working next to a flame. Wax must always be melted in bains-marie style, because if it is fused in a pot in direct contact with the flame, not only does it produce a large amount of smoke but it is also easily flammable. Should the wax start to smoke, turn off the heat source and leave to cool. Should it catch fire, cover the pot with a lid. Do not use water because when in contact with water, molten wax reacts like boiling oil: it produces dangerous splutters. Never pour molten wax down drains or sinks. Should some wax end up on your clothes or on fabrics, leave to cool, and cover with a sheet of paper and iron.
If you dirty your worktop or the surface of your furniture, leave to cool before scraping with a knife.
To remove any wax left in the containers, leave to soak in hot water. Once the water has cooled, the wax will float to the surface. Drain and save for another project.

THE WICK

Cut a wick of the desired length. Hold it with a skewer and immerse it in molten wax for a few seconds. Remove and pull it taut, then leave to cool on a sheet of paper in order to eliminate any excess wax. Insert one end of the skewer into a small metal ring, which will act as the base.

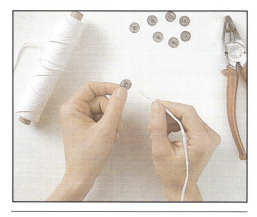

With a pair of pliers, squeeze the ring to prevent the wick from slipping out. Use some sealer to secure the wick to the base of the mold, then place a skewer across the mold and tie the free end of the wick around it, making sure it falls perfectly vertical. If you'd rather use pre-primed wicks, the market offers a wide range of different-sized wicks neatly packaged.

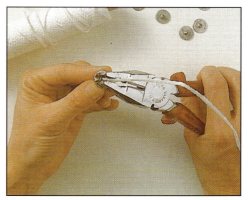

SCENTING WAX

A huge variety of essences to scent your candles are available in herbal shops. They are soluble in paraffin. These essences, which come in dropping bottles, have the perfume of aromatic flowers and herbs, and release delicious fragrances. Some of them (geranium and citronella) are good to fight mosquitoes, and come in handy in the summer, when dining in the open air. Dry flowers, aromatic herbs, and strips of dried citrus fruit peel may be left to infuse in hot wax for approximately 40 minutes. It is then up to you whether to remove them or leave them in the wax.

There are various techniques for scenting candles:
— You can either add a few drops of the chosen essence to the wax, mixing well to make sure it is well distributed. (Immerse the wick into the molten wax for approximately 20 minutes.)
— You can resort to the quickest method and squeeze some drops around the burning wick: the effect is more intense but less enduring.

MAKING CANDLES

DIPPED CANDLES

The dipping technique is an excellent starting point for learning how to make candles. It is not particularly difficult, nor does it require any specific equipment: the essentials can easily be found in your kitchen. Given that the candles will be 8" high, you must procure a container with a height of about 10" for melting the wax. The wax for dipped candles must be melted and kept at a temperature that does not make it either too thin or too thick. In the first case, the wax may slide away from the wick, while in the second case, it could form lumps on the surface of the candle. Experience will teach you to know when the wax is thick enough to adhere to the wick. Melt it until it has reached the temperature of approximately 160-175°F. Then turn off the heat.

You will need:

POT, ABOUT 8"
HEAT-PROOF GLASS
CONTAINER AT
LEAST 10" HIGH
WICK
PARAFFIN AND STEARIN
WOODEN SKEWER
NEWSPAPER
SCISSORS
CUTTER

Cut a piece of wick about 20" long and fold it into two equal parts. Holding it in the middle, immerse the free ends in hot wax for a few minutes and then carefully lift them out. Hang them on a wooden skewer, placed horizontally so that the two halves fall straight. Leave to dry. To prevent drops of hot wax from spilling on the table, cover the latter with some newspaper.

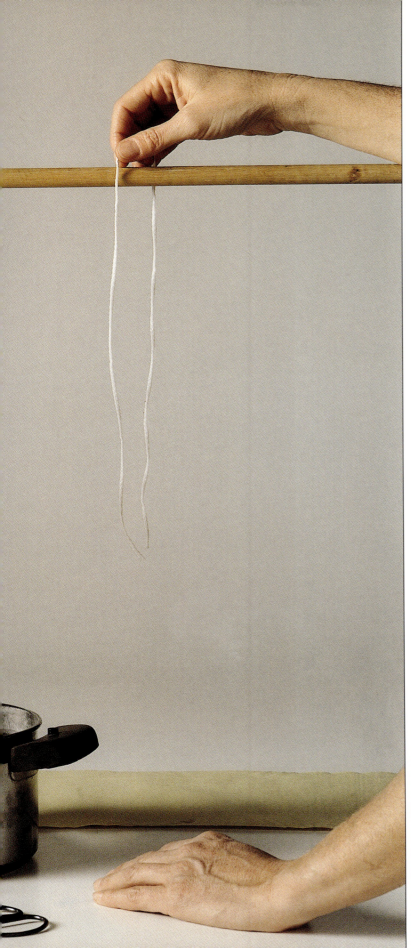

Immerse the wick several times to increase the thickness of the wax. When you have reached the desired thickness, you will have two elegant cone-shaped tapers. Use the cutter to trim the base of the candles and to eliminate, if necessary, the drop of wax left on the bottom.

MAKING CANDLES

There are two ways of making colored candles using the dipping technique:
1) Immerse the wick several times into the molten max (previously dyed);
2) Immerse a white candle into a pre-prepared mixture of dyed wax.

The intensity of the color depends on the number of dips. To make partially colored candles, dip only one part of the candle into the dye.

TWISTED CANDLES

With only a few light touches and the help of as simple of a tool as the rolling pin, you can mold dipped candles in elegant, sinuous forms.

YOU WILL NEED:

POT 8" HIGH
HEAT-PROOF GLASS CYLINDER AT LEAST 10" HIGH
WICK
PARAFFIN AND STEARIN
WOODEN STICK
NEWSPAPER
SCISSORS
CUTTER
WOODEN ROLLING PIN
HAIR-DRYER

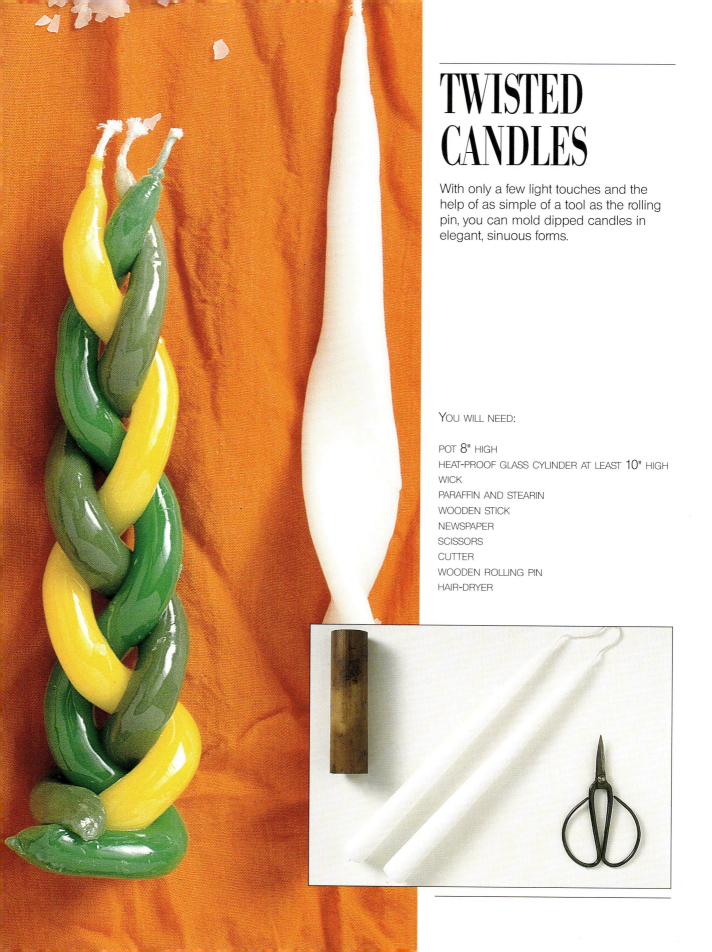

Make a candle using the dipping
technique. Before it cools down completely,
place it on your worktop and, with a rolling
pin, flatten the bottom half slightly. Holding
the two ends of the strip firmly, begin
twisting it.
If you have difficulty manipulating the
candle, you can heat it slightly with a hair
dryer. Should small cracks appear, immerse
it for a very short time into the molten wax.
Remove and leave to cool.

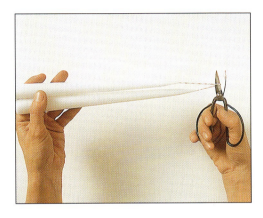

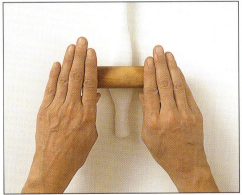

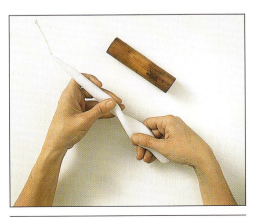

BEESWAX

In the old days, beeswax candles were made exclusively for the Church and the aristocracy. This was because they were very expensive and therefore well out of the reach of the common people. Even today beeswax is more expensive than paraffin, and is also more difficult to work with.

A substance with a very characteristic scent, beeswax melts at a temperature of about 150°F. It is available on the market in its natural colors, brown and yellow, or in white, if subjected to air bleaching or to industrial methods. Leave beeswax candles to "season" for approximately two years and place them in the fridge prior to being used.

Beeswax can be purchased in honeycomb, patterned sheets (8 x 16").

The sheets can either be honey yellow (the natural color of beeswax) or dyed in a wide range of hues, allowing you to set your creativity in motion when candle-making.

They can be cut, rolled up, or used to coat simple candles. They are perfect for a thousand different uses.

A useful tip: to prevent the wax from cracking, it is advisable to heat the sheet well with a hair-dryer before getting down to work.

YOU WILL NEED:

TWO SHEETS OF
DIFFERENT-COLORED
BEESWAX (8 x 16")
WICK
SCISSORS
CUTTER
RULER
HAIR-DRYER

Take two sheets of different-colored beeswax (8 x 16") and with a cutter, cut one sheet along the diagonal line, and the other along a straight line parallel to this, but about ⅛" further in.

You will obtain two rectangle triangles. Overlap them so that their sides coincide.

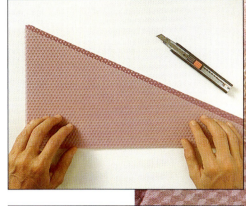

Now cut a wick about 10" long. Superimpose the two triangles so that the bigger one overlaps the smaller one.

Place the wick along the short side of the triangles. Heat with a hair-dryer to soften a little, and roll the sheets firmly around the wick.

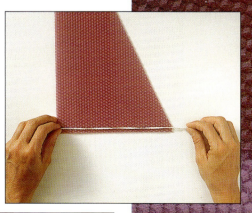

Perform this operation extremely carefully because the sheet could break.

Remember that the biggest sheet must remain on the inside of the roll to be molded.

Once finished rolling the sheet of wax, press the last piece (the most external one) slightly so as to secure it to the cone.

The heat of your fingers will be enough for the bottom part of the candle to adhere well. With a pair of scissors, trim the wick.

RAINBOW CANDLES

To make these multi-colored candles, you can use the wax of half burnt candles: melt it bains-marie style and remove the wick. Arranged on tree-like structures, these colorful candles will create a great effect.

YOU WILL NEED:

GLASS JARS
WAX
POT TO USE BAINS-
MARIE STYLE
WAX PASTELS
WICKS WITH BASES
SEALER
WOODEN SKEWERS
SCISSORS
DUSTER
GRATER
HALF BURNT CANDLES
PAINTBRUSH
THERMOMETER

Procure some poor quality glass jars of different shapes and sizes—at the end of the work, they will be broken.

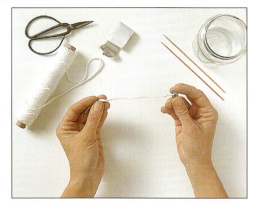

Prepare an equal amount of waxed wicks, complete with metal base.

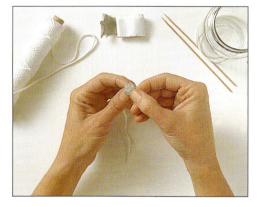

Secure them to the bottom of the jar with some sealer.

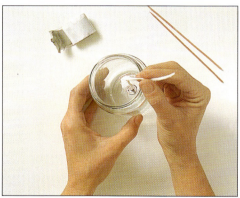

Tie the free end of the wick to a skewer placed across the edges of the jar. Use wax pastels to color the candles.

Grate or crumble a wax pastel and melt it in hot wax, mixing well until the color is homogeneous. Repeat this operation with the other pastels. Then pour a small quantity of colored wax into a jar and leave to cool. Then add a different color wax. Proceed in this manner with all the colors you have prepared in order to obtain layers of different hues. For the wax to cool rapidly, immerse the glass jar in a container full of water and ice, or leave in the refrigerator.

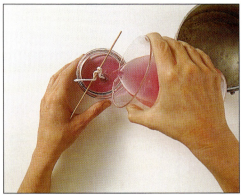

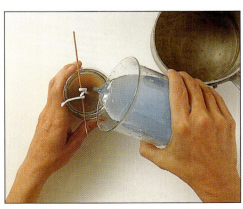

Should a hole form in line with the wick, fill it with a small quantity of very hot wax, naturally of the same color. Once the wax is completely cool, wrap the jar in a cloth and break it by forcefully tapping the base with a hammer. Unwrap the cloth and with the aid of a paintbrush, extract all the fragments of glass stuck on the surface of the candle. If you'd like to make these candles with leftover wax, melt partially burnt candles in bains-marie style.

CANDLES IN MOLDS

MOLDS

Molds to make strange-shaped candles, for reproducing all sorts of fruits or geometric shapes are used in different sizes.

Molds made of various materials such as glass, metal, plastic, and rubber (these last two are the most common) are available on the market. Plastic molds usually come in the shape of a ball, a cylinder, or a cone. They are made up of two separable halves, which fit perfectly over each other, and with an opening at the top through which to pour the wax. To obtain more intricate and complex shapes, you can use rubber molds, which are soft and elastic, thereby making it easier to extract the candles once set.

Do not use stearin with these molds because it is corrosive. All containers, which resist the melting temperature of wax (320°F), can be used as candle molds: milk bottles, ice-cream tubs, molds for sand, glass jars, and yogurt tubs.

Make sure that the mouth of your container is big enough to allow extracting the candle; otherwise it'll have to be broken open.

RUBBER MOLDS

Y<small>OU WILL NEED</small>:

RUBBER MOLD
(L<small>EMON</small>)
YELLOW PARAFFIN
POT FOR BAINS-MARIE
WICK
WOODEN SKEWERS
TAPESTRY NEEDLE
LIQUID DISH
DETERGENT
PIECE OF CARD
SCISSORS
THERMOMETER
FUNNEL
SMALL CANDLE

Heat the tip of the tapestry needle on your heat source.

Prick the end of the mold. The wick will be inserted with the tip of the needle.

To make it easier to extract the candle, coat the inside of the mold with a drop of liquid dish detergent.

At this point, insert the wick into the prepared hole.

You'll need something to support the mold, and this you can easily make by cutting a circle, whose diameter measures the same as that of the mold, in the center of a piece of cardboard.

Insert the mold into the cut circle, and then tie the free end of the wick to a wooden skewer that has been laid across the rims of the mold. Place the whole work in a suitable container.

Melt the paraffin and colored yellow in bains-marie style. Once it has reached 320°F, pour it into the mold with the aid of a funnel. Leave to cool and then fill the hole formed near the wick with hot paraffin.

Now stretch the border of the mold and turn the rubber shape upside down to extract the candle. By using this same method, you can make colorful candles in the shape of apples, mandarins, and watermelons.

PLASTIC MOLDS

YOU WILL NEED:

PLASTIC MOLD (TULIP)
COLORED WAX
POT FOR BAINS-MARIE
WICK WITH BASE
SCISSORS AND FUNNEL
PEGS
CUTTER
WOODEN SKEWERS
ADHESIVE TAPE
SHEET OF GREEN WAX
VESSEL CONTAINING SAND

Make a hole at the base of one of the two halves, of the mold, in order to pour in the wax. Secure the wick to the top of the mold with some adhesive tape, then pull it taut and out through the hole.

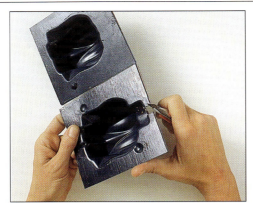

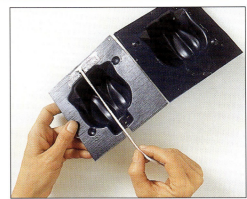

Seal the mold and block it in place with some clothes pins. Then insert it upright in a dry sand bath. Pour dyed molten wax (do not exceed 194°F) into the mold with the aid of a funnel.

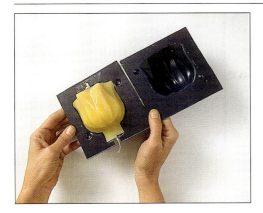

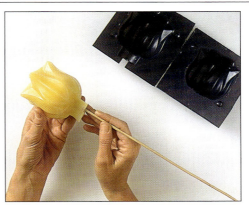

Leave to cool and fill up as required. When it has completely cooled, open the mold to extract the candle. With a cutter, pare away the wax left along the jointure.

To complete the tulip, insert a skewer (as the stem), and prepare some leaves to mold on the base of the flower, by cutting them from an ⅛" thick sheet of green wax.

GEOMETRICAL SHAPES

YOU WILL NEED:

WAX
POT
WICK
SCISSORS
FUNNEL
PLASTIC MOLD
ADHESIVE TAPE
WOODEN SKEWER
CUTTER
NYLON STOCKING

Make sure that the dovetailing mold, in the shape of a ball, is dry and clean. Place the wick along the mold lengthwise.

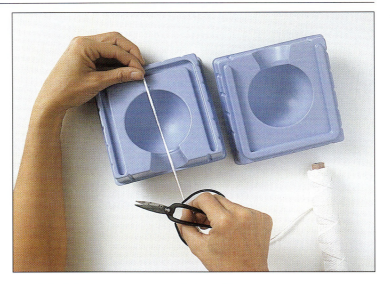

Secure the wick in the appropriate groove with some adhesive tape.

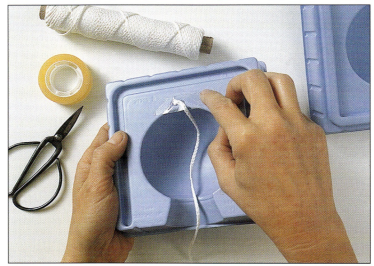

Seal the two halves of the mold, and extract the free end of the wick through the opening used to pour in the wax.

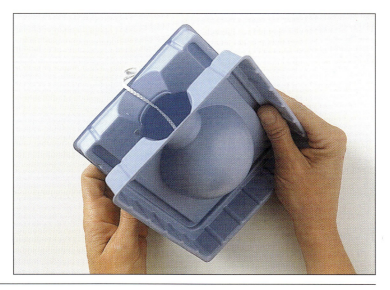

Secure the wick to the wooden skewer placed across the rims of the mold. Melt the wax bains-marie style and pour it into the mold. Make sure the wick is in the middle of the hole. Leave the wax to cool and then fill up again as needed.

Open the mold carefully and extract the candle.

With a cutter, pare away any wax left along the jointure. To remove fingerprints and haloes, wipe the candle with a nylon stocking.

WITH A LITTLE IMAGINATION...

*Depicted on these pages are some other types
of plastic molds:
below, a mold for making long, elongated candles;
on the left, a thin mold for making small, ornamental candles.*

*Pour the wax into the molds and leave to set for about half
an hour. Cut a wick 1½" longer than the candle and position
it in the middle of the wax, while it is still soft. To extract the
candle, tap the back of the mold gently. It is also possible to
position the wick once the candle is completed, by inserting it
through a hole made with the red-hot tip of a tapestry needle.*

KITCHEN MOLDS

You will probably find containers that can be transformed into molds among your kitchenware. Biscuit and custard molds, for example, are ideal for making small, simple, cake-shaped candles, or even romantic floating candles. Here are a few useful tips to help you use these containers as molds: if their shapes make it difficult to extract the candle, coat the inside with a few drops of liquid dish detergent. Then place the wax in the refrigerator to cool. If you'd rather have a candle shaped like the mold turned upside down, perforate a hole for the wick at the base of the container.

Y<small>OU WILL NEED</small>:

PLASTIC OR METAL
CONTAINERS
WAX
POT
WICK
SCISSORS
TAPESTRY NEEDLE

If you are using a plastic container, perforate a hole at the center of the base with the red-hot tip of a tapestry needle. Once the wick has been inserted, seal well to prevent the wax from spilling out.

FLOATING CANDLES

If you are using metal molds, such as those used for making biscuits, perforate a hole for the wick directly at the base of the candle using the red-hot tip of a needle.

With small biscuit molds, it is possible to make dainty little floating candles to place in glass bowls full of water. The effect is a very attractive play of light.

Given that the specific weight of wax is inferior to that of water, any candle whose base is greater than its height can float on water.

ICE CUBES

Candles, especially large ones, made by immersing ice cubes in hot wax are a great effect. You can use one-quart milk cartons as molds.

YOU WILL NEED:

ONE-QUART MILK CARTON
COLORED WAX
POT
WICK WITH APPROPRIATE BASE
WOODEN SKEWER
CUTTER
SCISSORS

Cut off the top part of the milk carton and use the remaining part as your mold. Prepare a wick, secure it to the base of the carton, and tie its free end to the usual wooden skewer.

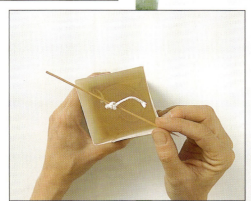

Pour some of the molten wax of your chosen color into the carton up to about 1", to get a rather thick base. Leave to cool.

Before the wax sets completely, drop in a few ice cubes, better if of different sizes.

Fill the mold completely with the remaining wax. As the wax cools, the ice cubes will melt. Cut the carton: water will spill out and where the ice cubes once were, there will be irregular, highly decorative cavities.

MAKING MOLDS

Irregular surfaces of a corrugated texture are ideal to use as the coating of candle molds. The rubber used to cover floors, whether with bubbles or striped, is perfect for this purpose.

YOU WILL NEED:

STRIP OF CORRUGATED RUBBER
ADHESIVE TAPE
LID OF A JAM JAR
POT
WICK WITH APPROPRIATE BASE
SCISSORS
CUTTER
WOODEN SKEWERS
SEALER
LIQUID DISH DETERGENT
SAND BATH

Take a strip of soft rubber about 8" and bend it to form a cylinder, making sure the embossed surface remains on the inside. To establish the width of the base, use the lid of a jam jar.

Seal the cylinder along the seam where the edges meet, with some adhesive tape. Then add the lid of the jam jar as the base and secure one end of the cylinder with more adhesive tape.

Coat the inside of the mold with a few drops of liquid dish detergent. Place the wick, complete with its base, in the center of the mold. Then tie the free end of the wick to a skewer positioned across the rims of the cylinder.

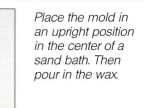

Place the mold in an upright position in the center of a sand bath. Then pour in the wax.

Leave to cool and refill it every now and again. Once the wax has cooled completely, remove the lid acting as the base.

Now, extract the candle from the mold, using a cutter to remove the adhesive tape sealing the cylinder. The result will be a candle with attractive vertical embossed stripes.

CANDLE-HOLDERS

TERRACOTTA VASES

Simple terracotta vases can become original candle-holders, which can be displayed in a garden or terrace to attractively illuminate a hidden corner.

YOU WILL NEED:

TERRACOTTA VASE
WAX PASTEL
EQUIPMENT
FOR MELTING WAX
BAINS-MARIE STYLE
WICK
SEALER
WOODEN SKEWERS
SCISSORS

Take a terracotta vase (should it have a hole at the base; seal this). Secure the wick to the center of the vase and pull it taut. Tie the free end of the wick to the wooden skewer placed across the rims of the vase.

Melt some wax and color it by crumbling in a wax pastel. Then pour the wax into the vase.

Leave it to cool and top it up with more wax until you have obtained a smooth, even surface. You can choose different-sized holders in which to pour the wax dyed in warm summer hues.

GLASS HOLDERS

Drinking glasses, whether thick or thin, colored or transparent, can be filled the same way as the terracotta vases. The technique is the same, but make sure that the wax is not too hot (329°F) when being poured, because the glass could break. If the holder is very large, you could decorate the candle by dropping in brilliantine, stars, or plasticine.

CANDLE-HOLDERS

USING SAND

Sand, a natural element full of charm,
is ideal to use as a candle-holder,
particularly in the summer. After being
gently sprinkled onto the still soft wax,
the grains of sand will shine
in the reflection of the burning flame.

YOU WILL NEED:

CONTAINER FULL
OF SAND
STAR-SHAPED MOLD
COLORED WAX
POT
WICK COMPLETE
WITH BASE
WOODEN SKEWER
SCISSORS

Select a wide but shallow container, fill it with sand, and dampen it with some water. Press the mold onto the sand to leave a clearly cut imprint.

Remove the mold. Place the wick, complete with its base, in the center of the imprint and secure its free end to a wooden skewer placed across the rims of the container.

Pour the colored wax, while it is still very hot, into the imprint. When in contact with the damp sand, the wax will solidify. Leave to cool for a couple of hours, then extract the candle by digging into the sand.

SHELL HOLDERS

Ideal for illuminating richly set tables
in the summer, shell holders create a very
evocative ambience. They are very easy
to make. The most important thing is
to have on hand shells of the right shape,
which can be collected when taking walks
on the beach during the summer.

YOU WILL NEED:

SHELLS
WAX
POT
WICK COMPLETE
WITH BASE
WOODEN SKEWERS
SCISSORS
GLUE

Thoroughly wash and dry the shells. Secure the wick with a drop of glue to the base of the shell.

Cut the wick to the right size and tie its free end to a piece of wooden skewer placed across the rims of the shell.

Melt the wax bains-marie style and pour it carefully into the shell. Repeat this operation for the other half of the shell.

Leave the wax to cool. Do not move the shell in order to prevent unattractive smudges from forming.

HOLDERS FROM NATURAL PRODUCTS

Any kind of fruit that has a resistant shell can be transformed into an unusual candle-holder. A coconut, with its wood-like husk, was used for this project. It was first emptied of its milk and pulp, then left to dry. Finally, it was filled with wax.

YOU WILL NEED:

COCONUT
WHITE WAX
POT
WICK
SEALER
WOODEN SKEWERS
THERMOMETER
CORD
SCISSORS
HAMMER

With a hammer, break the coconut into two equal parts. Empty it of its milk and pulp and then clean the inside of the husk thoroughly.

Place the two halves on your worktop so that they don't move. Secure a wick to the center of both halves and tie the free ends to wooden skewers placed across the rims of the husks.

Prepare some white wax, bring it to a temperature of 165°F, and pour into the two husks.

With some cord prepare a simple support, as depicted on this page, for hanging the candle in the garden, or on the terrace.

Any fruit with a resistant shell can be transformed into a candle-holder. Clean the inside of the shell thoroughly and, after having positioned the wick, pour in the hot dyed wax. Leave to cool.

A SILVER GLOW

Candles in tin containers are ideal for being used outdoors because they protect the flame from the evening air. You can use white or dyed wax to obtain ever-different reflections.

YOU WILL NEED:

TINS

WAX

POT

WICK

WOODEN SKEWERS

LONG NAILS

PRICK

HAMMER

PENCIL AND RUBBER

RULER

SHEET OF PAPER

SCISSORS

ADHESIVE TAPE

Take a tin soup can. Open it, remove the lid completely, and empty it of its contents. Cut away the strip of paper around the tin and clean thoroughly. Measure the circumference of the base and the height of the tin.

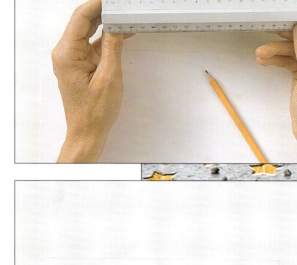

On a sheet of paper, draw a rectangle with these measurements to represent the base and height of the tin respectively. Begin decorating with simple designs at about 1½" or 2" from the base and continue to the top.

Wrap the sheet of paper around the tin and secure it along the seam where the edges meet with some adhesive tape.

Take a nail and place it on one of the drawings. With a hammer, make some holes along the lines of the decoration, distancing them at about ³/₄ or 1" from each other.

Once completed, remove the sheet of paper. Use a prick to widen the holes. Secure the wick to the base of the tin, pull it taut, and tie its free end around a skewer placed across the rims of the container.

Pour some molten wax into the tin to fill 1½" or 2". Leave to cool until the candle is set.

MAGIC LANTERNS

Once lit, these original glass lanterns create an "Arabian Nights" effect.

YOU WILL NEED:

GLASS JAR
COLORS FOR GLASS
TUBE OF GOLD PASTE
FOR GLASS
PAINTBRUSH
LATEX GLOVES
WHITE WAX
POT
WICK
SMALL NIGHT LIGHT
CANDLE

Glass jars can easily be transformed into small lanterns. With a paintbrush, coat the outside of the jar with a layer of color. Leave to dry completely. Wear latex gloves throughout this operation.

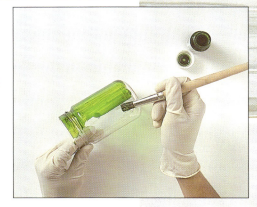

Using a tube of gold paste, specific for glass and complete with a little beak, draw patterns on the jar.

Wait until the paste has dried before pouring in the wax to fill about 1" of the jar. Insert the wick.

As an alternative, you could place a small purchased night light in the jar.

CANDLES MADE WITH UNHEATED WAX

Candles can also be made with unheated wax. To make, use wax powders made from uniform micro-crystals of various colors.

Take a rather large glass, if possible a goblet.
Tilt the glass towards you and pour in layers of different colored wax.

You can alternate oblique layers with horizontal ones, combining the colors.

Insert the wick down the center, and see that it remains in an upright position. Continue to pour the wax until you have almost completely filled the glass.

If necessary, trim the wick with a pair of scissors.

YOU WILL NEED:

WAX POWDER IN
DIFFERENT COLORS
WICK
DRINKING GLASS
SCISSORS

The micro-crystals making up the powder float, therefore, you can make candles in which you alternate layers of wax with layers of water, creating an effect that most strikes your imagination.

Half fill a glass with cold water. Slowly pour in the first layer of dyed–powdered wax.

Holding the glass still, pour in more powdered wax and then place the wick in the center. If necessary, trim the wick with a pair of scissors.

DECORATED CANDLES

DRIED FLOWERS

If you have the patience to pick small flowers and simple field herbs, than you can enjoy the satisfaction of seeing them "flower again" by using them to decorate lively, spring candles.

YOU WILL NEED:

DRIED FLOWERS
TEASPOON
WHITE OR NATURAL
HUED CANDLES
PARAFFIN
POT
SHEET OF PAPER
TWEEZERS
SCENTED ESSENCES
SMALL NIGHT LIGHT
CANDLE

Arrange some flowers harmoniously onto a sheet of paper. With a pair of tweezers, lift the flowers one at a time and place them onto the candle.

Heat the back of a teaspoon over a flame, and use it to press the flower to the candle until it is firmly attached.

Repeat this operation with the remaining flowers, distributing them well around the candle.

Once completed, hold the candle by the wick and immerse it quickly in very hot paraffin.

In this way, the floral decoration will be "sealed" to the surface of the candle.

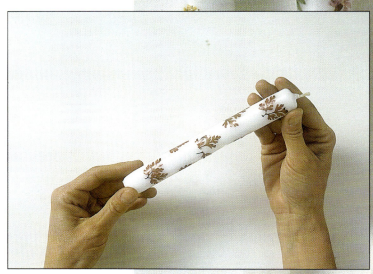

If, when lit, you would like the candle to give off the scent of the flowers decorating it, add a few drops of essence to the molten wax or directly onto the wick.

CARVED CANDLES

The tools generally used to carry out this decorative technique are those used to carve wood, heated over a flame. Carved candles can then either be colored by immersion, in which case the decoration will be white, or painted with various layers of colors, whereby the candles will take on different shades of color.

YOU WILL NEED:

WHITE CANDLE
TEMPERA COLORS
PAINTBRUSH
SAUCER
CUTTER
HAIR-DRYER
LIQUID DISH DETERGENT

Mix the tempera colors with a drop of soap so that it will adhere better to the wax. Then with a paintbrush, paint vertical stripes on the white candle, alternating between yellow and red.

Once the colors have dried, paint the whole candle with black tempera. Before continuing with the work, make sure that the color has dried completely.

Delicately carve the surface of the candle with a cutter, creating floral motifs. From the carved lines of the etched flowers will appear the colors of the first layer.

Alternatively, you could coat the candle by immersing it in layers of different-colored wax, and then carve the decorations with a cutter. To eliminate any excess wax, soften the candle by heating it with a hair-dryer.

TEMPERA DECORATIONS

It is possible to make an endless range of decorations on candles by using simple tempera colors. Depicted on these pages are only some suggestions, which can be enriched by giving your imagination free reign. Dab the color with small sponges, or use a paintbrush to paint floral or geometric motifs, or even details from famous pictures.

YOU WILL NEED:

WHITE CANDLE
TEMPERA COLORS
(INCLUDING GOLD)
TWO ROUND-TIPPED
PAINTBRUSHES (A BIG
AND A SMALL ONE)
LIQUID DISH DETERGENT
TEMPERA COLORS
SAUCER

Remember that tempera colors adhere better to the surface of a candle if mixed with a drop of liquid dish detergent.

Candles can be decorated with ornamental, geometric, or floral motifs. To make bright Christmas candles, paint delicate decorations in gold with a fine-tipped paintbrush over a red wax base.

When the decoration has dried, begin to paint the sides of the candle with the ornamental motifs you prefer.

Besides the traditional decorative star-shaped motif, you could paint wavy lines, geometric shapes, or evocative gold moons.

STAMPED CANDLES

To decorate a candle quickly, here is a simple technique; stamping. Choose stamps of the most suitable material and size. In this way, you will obtain colorful decorations based on a combination of repeated patterns.

YOU WILL NEED:

CANDLE
WOODEN OR PLASTIC
STAMP
INK AND PAD
LIQUID DISH DETERGENT
SPONGE
TEMPERA COLORS
PAINTBRUSH
SAUCER
STAMPED RUBBER
PLASTIC BRUSHES
COMB

Use a small sponge to coat the candle with liquid dish detergent. Ink the pad and press your chosen stamp onto it. Then stamp the candle. Repeat this operation, distributing the decoration over the whole surface of the candle.

The smaller the stamp, the more delicate the designs are on the candle.

To decorate with repeated motifs (frottage), besides stamps, you could also use other surfaces to dip in the dye, such as a paintbrush, small plastic brushes, combs, or pieces of printed rubber.

DECORATING WITH SPONGES

This type of decoration does not require a lot of material: tempera colors and small sponges with which to dab the colors on the candle complete your tool kit.

You will obtain an irregular and uneven result. Your candles will become more unique as you learn how to mix and match different colors.

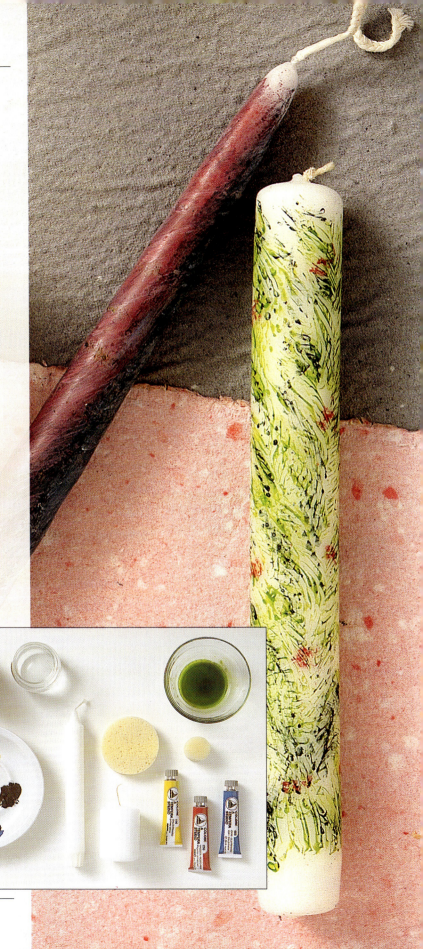

YOU WILL NEED:

WHITE CANDLES
TEMPERA COLORS
(INCLUDING GOLD)
SAUCER
VARIOUS-SIZED
SPONGES
LIQUID DISH DETERGENT
PAINTBRUSH

Use a paintbrush to coat the candle with a drop of liquid dish detergent, which will act as a base.

Dip the damp sponge into the tempera color, previously diluted in water with a drop of liquid dish detergent.

Dab the candle lightly with the sponge, and then repeat this operation with another color. Let your imagination run wild, using the endless range of hues to decorate the candles with a harmonious play of colors.

STENCIL MOTIFS

You will need:

CANDLE
SPRAY COLORS
FOR STENCILS
(INCLUDING GOLD)
SPRAY FIXATIVE
STENCILS
PAPER DOILIES
LEAVES

Attach some stencil paper with a decorative motif, a paper doily, or some leaves to the candle and fix them to the wax with adhesive spray. Remember to read the instructions carefully before spraying and to protect your worktop with some paper.

Once the stencil has been fixed to the candle, spray the paint evenly. It is advisable to spray in a well-ventilated room.

Leave to dry over night before removing the stencil. The candle will be decorated in the negative.

SILVER AND GOLD DECORATIONS

Both lead and gold pastes are generally used for decorating glass, but they are also very effective when used on candles. Lead and gold paste are both available on the market and come in tubes complete with a long narrow–tipped beak. As a consequence, they are perfect when it comes to making minute decorations, rich in detail, which would be difficult to obtain with a paintbrush. The patterns drawn with this paste will remain slightly embossed on the candle.

YOU WILL NEED:

COLORED CANDLES
TUBE OF LEAD PASTE
TUBE OF GOLD PASTE

This paste is easy to use: it adheres perfectly to the wax and doesn't come off when dry.

Take a tube of lead paste, complete with beak, and begin carrying out simple decorations on the top part of the candle. Proceed until the whole candle has been decorated, making sure not to touch it with your hands.
Leave to dry for a couple of hours.

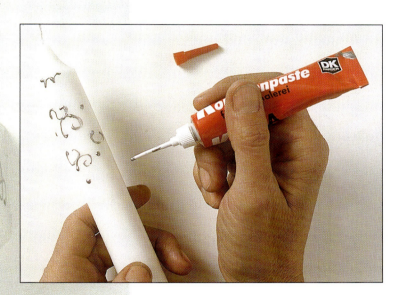

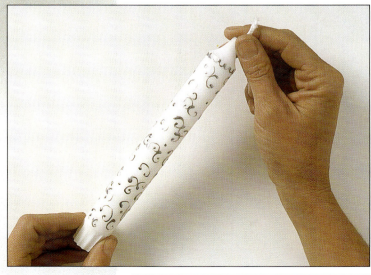

DELIGHTFUL TRANSFERS

There is a wealth of transferable decorations, which give the same effects as decoupage, available on the market. These decorations can be applied on different surfaces such as: wax, acrylic materials, carton, wood, metal, and glass, and the kit generally comes complete with a spatula for transferring them.

ADVENT CANDLES

The advent candle burns slowly, marking the passage of time from the 1st of December to the 24th, Christmas Eve. Thus the candle is an example of a time marking candle, and it highlights the passing of the days during the sacred period of Advent.

YOU WILL NEED:

CANDLE ABOUT
20" LONG
RED TRANSFERABLE
NUMBERS
TRACING PAPER
PENCIL AND RULER
WOODEN SPATULA
RIBBON
SHEETS OF
COLORED WAX
SMALL RED
METAL STARS

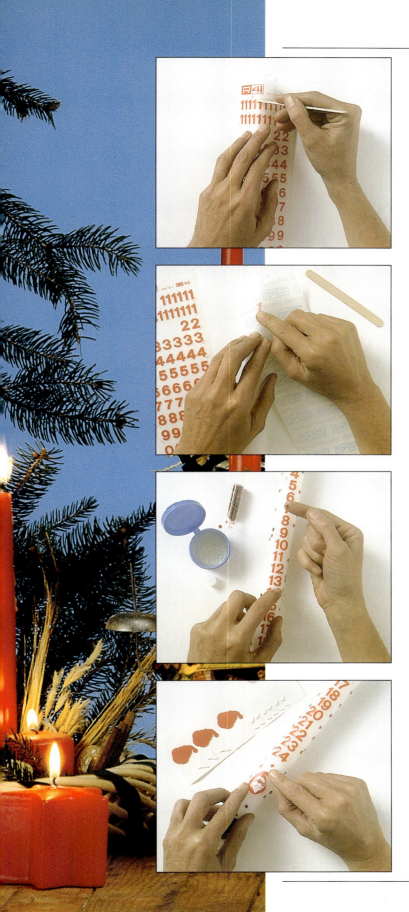

Divide the candle into 24 equal parts lengthwise, and then position the corresponding adhesive numbers. After having cleaned the surface of the candle carefully, remove the protective paper from the transfers.

Place the transfer with number 1 at the top of the candle. With a wooden spatula, press lightly so that the number adheres well to the candle. Always press the transfer from the center outwards.

To ensure that the number adheres well to the candle, place a sheet of tracing paper between your fingers and the transfer, and press lightly with the other 23 transferable numbers in a column beneath the number 1.

Finish off the candle by gluing on many red stars. To protect the decorations, immerse the candle into molten paraffin. Complete the effect by gluing on a small Santa Claus made from a sheet of wax and tie on a ribbon.

WAX APPLICATIONS

YOU WILL NEED:

A BIG CANDLE
CUTTER
HAIR-DRYER

FOR THE SHEETS
OF WAX
KITCHEN BOWL
WHITE OR
COLORED WAX
POT
SMALL PAINTBRUSH
LIQUID DISH DETERGENT
BISCUIT MOLDS

To make small wax decorations for applying on the candle, prepare a thin sheet of wax. Use a small paintbrush to coat the base of a rather wide Pyrex dish.

Pour some white or colored molten wax into the dish until you have a very thin, even layer (about ⅛").

Leave to cool. You will now have a thin sheet of wax from which to cut out, with the aid of a cutter or metal biscuit molds, various decorations for the candle.

To render the shapes soft, malleable, and ready to adhere well to the candle, heat them with a hair-dryer.

Place the wax decorations onto the candle, and press them lightly in the desired position.

Apply all the decorations in this manner until the candle is complete.

RIBBONS

Raffia fibers, trimming or silk ribbons, and cotton nets are all materials which can be used to coat candles to suit your tastes.

<small>YOU WILL NEED:</small>

CANDLES OF
DIFFERENT COLORS
VINYL GLUE
CORD
SCISSORS
TRIMMINGS
COTTON NETS
SILK RIBBONS
RAFFIA FIBERS
PARAFFIN
POT

To decorate candles with a cord, start from the base: spread some glue on a small part of the candle surface and place the cord on it (for this candle, a soft, thin–colored paper cord was used), pressing lightly with your fingers so that the cord adheres to the candle well.

Work upwards from the point where you have spread the glue, wrapping each turn of the cord as near to the last as possible.

Once completed, dip the candle quickly in molten paraffin to secure the decoration. Different types of trimmings can be combined in this way to make attractive decorations.

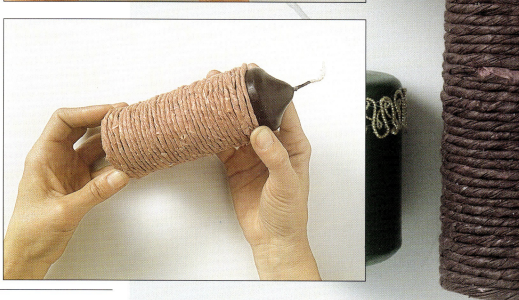

SEED COATED CANDLES

YOU WILL NEED:

CANDLE
MEXICAN BEAN SEEDS
LENTILS
COFFEE
VINYL GLUE
PARAFFIN
POT
WOODEN SKEWERS
SMALL PAINTBRUSH

Spread a light layer of glue onto the candle, working from the top to the bottom.

Use a wooden skewer to help you carry out this operation.

Arrange the small, dark Mexican beans onto the glue in an even fashion.

Proceed in this manner until you have coated the entire candle.

Once finished, leave the glue to dry completely.

To secure the seeds firmly to the wax, immerse the candle in very hot paraffin (holding the candle by the wick). If you want the seeds to remain clearly visible, dip very briefly to prevent them from being covered by a film of paraffin.

ENFOLDED IN NATURE

A large candle lends itself well to being coated with elements found in nature. Bark found in the woods, wheat or oak ears, flax and lavender flowers, cinnamon, and bamboo sticks can all be used as natural holders for candles, the latter being preferably of wax.

YOU WILL NEED:

LARGE CANDLE
WHEAT, OAT
OR BARLEY EARS
VINYL GLUE
ELASTICS
SCISSORS
NATURAL RAFFIA
FIBERS
PARAFFIN
POT
WOODEN SKEWERS

Take a large sized candle. Spread a strip of glue on a part of the candle with a wooden skewer, working from the top downwards.

Place some ears alongside each other on the glue, with the stems running up the candle and the ears well over its top border. Press slightly so that they adhere well.

Cut any stems protruding beyond the bottom border of the candle. Wrap an elastic band around them half–way up the candle.

Spread the glue onto the remaining surface and add more ears.

Insert them carefully inside the elastic, which serves to keep them firmly in place. Once the glue has dried, they will remain attached to the candle in the right position.

When the entire candle has been coated, leave to dry before removing the elastic. Tie the ears with some natural raffia fibers, ending off with a bow.

Trim the stems with a pair of scissors. Use this method to decorate candles with other natural elements.

The natural elements applied to these candles were all secured to the wax through a brief immersion in hot paraffin.

CORRUGATED CARDBOARD

YOU WILL NEED:

CANDLE
CORRUGATED
CARDBOARD
VINYL GLUE
SCISSORS
CUTTER
CORD
PENCIL AND RUBBER
RULER

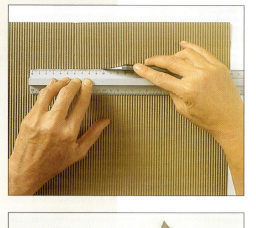

Cut a rectangle, measuring the circumference of the base and height of the candle, from the corrugated cardboard.

Secure it around the candle with a some vinyl glue.

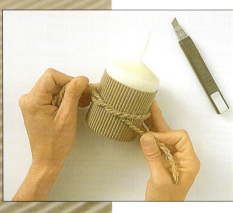

When the glue is completely dry, tie a piece of untreated cord around the candle.

Tie the cord into a decorative knot.

ENGRAVED CANDLES

To make elegant, carved candles it is advisable to use long, thin candles, made with the dipping technique.

YOU WILL NEED:

DIPPED CANDLE
WHITE OR COLORED WAX
POT
CUTTER
HAIR-DRYER

Take a white dipped candle, which still needs to be immersed in wax a couple of times to acquire the right size.

Immerse it twice in molten wax, and then leave it for a few minutes. Keep a hair-dryer ready for heating the surface of the candle when it needs to become more pliable.

Make a deep, slanting incision inwards with a cutter, pushing the blade downwards.

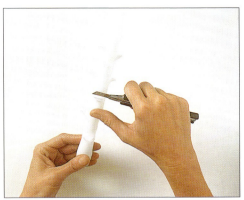

Press the cut layer of wax between your thumb and forefinger, and then curl the wax outwards. Proceed in this way until you have obtained many curling layers, each distanced from the other.

Rotate the candle clockwise and make more incisions all around, at different heights, remembering to heat the wax to prevent the curls from coming off.

To obtain an even more striking effect, use colored waxes. The more the candle is immersed in different colors, the more attractive is the decoration, as the curls will show up the hues of the underlying layers of wax.

PAPER LANTERNS

All you need to make evocative lanterns is a sheet of Japanese paper and a pair of scissors. You may either cut the sheet smaller or leave it as it is, and cut out small windows through which the light can shine.

Draw two lanterns on a sheet of Japanese paper. As this is woven with small vegetable fibers, flower petals, and strips of bark, this paper lends itself well to making individual lanterns.

Cut out the two halves of the lantern and join them along the edges, inserting two wooden skewers vertically.

You will have obtained a vaguely cylindrical shape. A glass jar holding a candle acts as the base of the lantern.

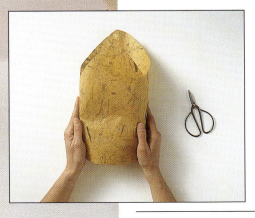

Choose different-colored papers to cut out windows or decorative geometrical or floral shapes, and so to transform the candles into evocative, enchanted castles.

YOU WILL NEED:

CANDLE
GLASS JAR
PENCIL AND SCISSORS
JAPANESE PAPER
WOODEN SKEWERS

CANDLES FOR EVERY OCCASION

EASTER

Easter eggs galore, and not only of chocolate: in the soft hues of spring, or decorated with many small, multicolored flowers, these candles will glitter on your table laid out to celebrate the feast.

CHRISTMAS

Using candles at Christmas is a tradition from the northern countries: in olden times, winter solstice, the darkest day of the year, was celebrated by brightening the sky with the little flames from candles, used as ornaments on the fir tree branches. Today fir tree green, red, and gold are a combination of colors, which have come to symbolize this feast day.

SAINT VALENTINE'S DAY

The main theme on Saint Valentine's Day is the heart; in different shades of red. The white flames and the red candle are a perfect match.

HALLOWEEN

Pumpkins galore with which to celebrate Halloween can be used as beguiling candle-holders. Orange candles with black decorations and flying bats complete your party.

BIRTHDAYS

A thousand colors should be used for a birthday party, with candles, of all sizes and colors, that have to be blown out in one breath!

INDEX

A

Advent candles, 126–127

B

Beeswax
  characteristics, 10
  making candles from,
  32–35
Birthday candles, 158

C

Candle-holders
  glass, 76
  magic lanterns, 92–94
  from natural products,
  84–86
  shells for, 82–83
  silver glow, 88–91
  terracotta vases, 72–74
  for unheated wax,
  96–98
  using sand for, 78–81
Carved candles,
  108–109
Christmas candles, 154
Coconut candle-holder,
  84–85
Colored candles, dip
  ping technique for, 28
Corrugated cardboard
  decorations, 146–147

D

Decorated candles
  for advent, 126–127
  carved, 108–109
  corrugated cardboard,
  146–147
  dried flowers, 102–106
  engraved, 148–149

with natural elements,
  140–144
paper lanterns,
  150–151
ribbons, 132–134
seed-coated, 136–139
silver and gold,
  122–123
sponge technique for,
  116–118
stamped, 112–115
stencil motifs, 120–121
tempera, 110–111
transfers, 124
wax applications for,
  128–131
Dipped candles, 24–28
Dried flowers, for
  candle decoration,
  102–106
Dye, wax, 16

E

Easter candles, 154
Engraved candles,
  148–149
Equipment, 12

F

Floating candles, 62
Fruit candle-holder, 86

G

Geometrically shaped
  candles, 54–57
Gold decorated candles,
  122–123

H

Halloween candles, 156

M

Materials, 10
Melting method, for wax,
  12, 15, 16
Molds, 44
  for floating candles, 62
  geometrically shaped,
  54–57
  ice cube technique,
  64–65
  kitchen, 60–61
  making, 66–69
  plastic, 50–53, 58–59
  rubber, 46–49
Multi-colored candles,
  36–40

N

Natural decorations,
  140–144

P

Paper lanterns, 150–151
Paraffin, 10

R

Rainbow candles,
  36–40
Ribbons, for candle
  decorations, 132–134

S

Safety precautions, 16
Saint Valentine's day
  candles, 156
Sand, using as candle-
  holder, 78–81
Scenting candles, 21
Seed-coated candles,
  136–139

Shell holders, 82–83
Silver decorated
  candles, 122–123
Silver glow
  candle-holder, 88–91
Sponge technique, for
  candle decoration,
  116–118
Stamped candles,
  112–115
Stearin, 10
Stencil motifs, for candle
  decoration, 120–121

T

Techniques. See also
  under specific types of
  candles
  basic, 9–22
Tempera decorations,
  110–111
Transfer decorations, 124
Twisted candles, 30–31

V

Valentine's day candles,
  156

W

Wax
  applications, for candle
  decorations, 128–131
  beeswax (See
  Beeswax)
  preparing, 15
  scenting, 21
  types, 10
  unheated, candles
  made from, 96–98
Wick, 10, 18–19